To:

_____

From:

_____

Date:

_____

DELIGHT YOURSELF IN THE LORD, AND HE WILL
GIVE YOU THE DESIRES OF YOUR HEART. PS. 37:4

THE LORD IS MY LIGHT AND MY SALVATION—WHOM
SHALL I FEAR? THE LORD IS THE STRONGHOLD OF MY
LIFE—OF WHOM SHALL I BE AFRAID? PS. 27:1

THE LORD HIMSELF GOES BEFORE YOU AND WILL
BE WITH YOU; HE WILL NEVER LEAVE YOU NOR
FORSAKE YOU. DEUT. 31:8

GOD IS WORKING IN YOU, GIVING YOU THE DESIRE TO
OBEY HIM AND THE POWER TO DO WHAT PLEASES HIM.

PHIL. 2:13

_____
_____
_____
_____
_____
_____
_____
_____
_____
_____
_____
_____
_____
_____
_____
_____
_____
_____
_____
_____
_____
_____
_____

I CAN DO EVERYTHING THROUGH CHRIST, WHO
GIVES ME STRENGTH. PHIL. 4:13

IF YOU WANT TO KNOW WHAT GOD WANTS YOU TO DO,
ASK HIM, AND HE WILL GLADLY TELL YOU. JAMES 1:5

CREATE IN ME A PURE HEART, O GOD, AND RENEW
A STEADFAST SPIRIT WITHIN ME. PS. 51:10

IF ANYONE IS IN CHRIST, HE IS A NEW CREATION;
THE OLD HAS GONE, THE NEW HAS COME! 2 COR. 5:17

CAST YOUR CARES ON THE LORD
AND HE WILL SUSTAIN YOU. PS. 55:22

THE LORD YOUR GOD IS WITH YOU, HE IS MIGHTY TO
SAVE. HE WILL TAKE GREAT DELIGHT IN YOU, HE WILL
QUIET YOU WITH HIS LOVE. ZEPH. 3:17

THE LORD IS FAITHFUL TO ALL HIS PROMISES
AND LOVING TOWARD ALL HE HAS MADE. PS. 145:13

IN YOU, O LORD, DO I PUT MY TRUST. PS. 71:1

"BE STRONG AND COURAGEOUS. . . . THE LORD YOUR GOD
WILL BE WITH YOU WHEREVER YOU GO." JOSH. 1:9

DEPEND ON THE LORD IN WHATEVER YOU DO,
AND YOUR PLANS WILL SUCCEED. PROV. 16:3

SINCE WE HAVE BEEN JUSTIFIED THROUGH FAITH,
WE HAVE PEACE WITH GOD THROUGH OUR
LORD JESUS CHRIST. ROM. 5:1

THE LORD IS MY ROCK, MY FORTRESS AND MY DELIVERER;
MY GOD IS MY ROCK, IN WHOM I TAKE REFUGE. PS. 18:2

"IF ANYONE WOULD COME AFTER ME, HE MUST DENY
HIMSELF AND TAKE UP HIS CROSS AND FOLLOW ME."

MATT. 16:24

THE WORD OF THE LORD IS RIGHT AND TRUE;
HE IS FAITHFUL IN ALL HE DOES. PS. 33:4

THE LORD IS MY STRENGTH, MY SHIELD FROM EVERY
DANGER. I TRUST IN HIM WITH ALL MY HEART. PS. 28:7

IN HIM WE HAVE REDEMPTION THROUGH HIS BLOOD,
THE FORGIVENESS OF SINS, IN ACCORDANCE WITH
THE RICHES OF GOD'S GRACE. EPH. 1:7

I TRUST IN YOUR UNFAILING LOVE. I WILL REJOICE
BECAUSE YOU HAVE RESCUED ME. PS. 13:5

LIVE A LIFE OF LOVE, JUST AS CHRIST LOVED US AND
GAVE HIMSELF UP FOR US. EPH. 5:2

"YOU WILL CALL UPON ME AND COME AND PRAY TO ME, AND I WILL LISTEN TO YOU. YOU WILL SEEK ME AND FIND ME WHEN YOU SEEK ME WITH ALL YOUR HEART." JER. 29:12–13

MY SOUL FINDS REST IN GOD ALONE;
MY SALVATION COMES FROM HIM. PS. 62:1

DELIGHT YOURSELF IN THE LORD, AND HE WILL
GIVE YOU THE DESIRES OF YOUR HEART. PS. 37:4

THE LORD IS MY LIGHT AND MY SALVATION—WHOM
SHALL I FEAR? THE LORD IS THE STRONGHOLD OF MY
LIFE—OF WHOM SHALL I BE AFRAID? PS. 27:1

THE LORD HIMSELF GOES BEFORE YOU AND WILL
BE WITH YOU; HE WILL NEVER LEAVE YOU NOR
FORSAKE YOU. DEUT. 31:8

GOD IS WORKING IN YOU, GIVING YOU THE DESIRE TO
OBEY HIM AND THE POWER TO DO WHAT PLEASES HIM.

PHIL. 2:13

I CAN DO EVERYTHING THROUGH CHRIST, WHO
GIVES ME STRENGTH. PHIL. 4:13

IF YOU WANT TO KNOW WHAT GOD WANTS YOU TO DO,
ASK HIM, AND HE WILL GLADLY TELL YOU. JAMES 1:5

CREATE IN ME A PURE HEART, O GOD, AND RENEW
A STEADFAST SPIRIT WITHIN ME. PS. 51:10

IF ANYONE IS IN CHRIST, HE IS A NEW CREATION;
THE OLD HAS GONE, THE NEW HAS COME! 2 COR. 5:17

CAST YOUR CARES ON THE LORD
AND HE WILL SUSTAIN YOU. PS. 55:22

THE LORD YOUR GOD IS WITH YOU, HE IS MIGHTY TO
SAVE. HE WILL TAKE GREAT DELIGHT IN YOU, HE WILL
QUIET YOU WITH HIS LOVE. ZEPH. 3:17

THE LORD IS FAITHFUL TO ALL HIS PROMISES
AND LOVING TOWARD ALL HE HAS MADE. PS. 145:13

IN YOU, O LORD, DO I PUT MY TRUST. PS. 71:1

"BE STRONG AND COURAGEOUS. . . . THE LORD YOUR GOD
WILL BE WITH YOU WHEREVER YOU GO." JOSH. 1:9

DEPEND ON THE LORD IN WHATEVER YOU DO,
AND YOUR PLANS WILL SUCCEED. PROV. 16:3

SINCE WE HAVE BEEN JUSTIFIED THROUGH FAITH,
WE HAVE PEACE WITH GOD THROUGH OUR
LORD JESUS CHRIST. ROM. 5:1

THE LORD IS MY ROCK, MY FORTRESS AND MY DELIVERER;
MY GOD IS MY ROCK, IN WHOM I TAKE REFUGE. PS. 18:2

"IF ANYONE WOULD COME AFTER ME, HE MUST DENY
HIMSELF AND TAKE UP HIS CROSS AND FOLLOW ME."
MATT. 16:24

THE WORD OF THE LORD IS RIGHT AND TRUE;
HE IS FAITHFUL IN ALL HE DOES. PS. 33:4

THE LORD IS MY STRENGTH, MY SHIELD FROM EVERY
DANGER. I TRUST IN HIM WITH ALL MY HEART. PS. 28:7

IN HIM WE HAVE REDEMPTION THROUGH HIS BLOOD,
THE FORGIVENESS OF SINS, IN ACCORDANCE WITH
THE RICHES OF GOD'S GRACE. EPH. 1:7

I TRUST IN YOUR UNFAILING LOVE. I WILL REJOICE
BECAUSE YOU HAVE RESCUED ME. PS. 13:5

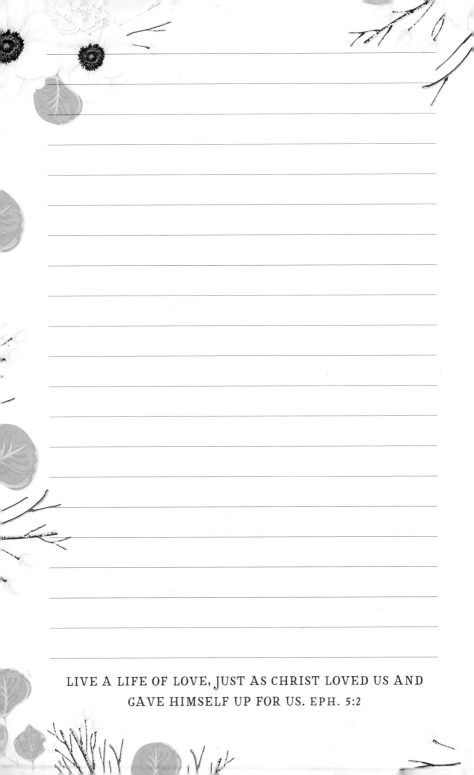

LIVE A LIFE OF LOVE, JUST AS CHRIST LOVED US AND
GAVE HIMSELF UP FOR US. EPH. 5:2

"YOU WILL CALL UPON ME AND COME AND PRAY TO ME, AND
I WILL LISTEN TO YOU. YOU WILL SEEK ME AND FIND ME
WHEN YOU SEEK ME WITH ALL YOUR HEART." JER. 29:12–13

MY SOUL FINDS REST IN GOD ALONE;
MY SALVATION COMES FROM HIM. PS. 62:1

DELIGHT YOURSELF IN THE LORD, AND HE WILL
GIVE YOU THE DESIRES OF YOUR HEART. PS. 37:4

THE LORD IS MY LIGHT AND MY SALVATION—WHOM
SHALL I FEAR? THE LORD IS THE STRONGHOLD OF MY
LIFE—OF WHOM SHALL I BE AFRAID? PS. 27:1

THE LORD HIMSELF GOES BEFORE YOU AND WILL
BE WITH YOU; HE WILL NEVER LEAVE YOU NOR
FORSAKE YOU. DEUT. 31:8

GOD IS WORKING IN YOU, GIVING YOU THE DESIRE TO
OBEY HIM AND THE POWER TO DO WHAT PLEASES HIM.

PHIL. 2:13

I CAN DO EVERYTHING THROUGH CHRIST, WHO
GIVES ME STRENGTH. PHIL. 4:13

IF YOU WANT TO KNOW WHAT GOD WANTS YOU TO DO,
ASK HIM, AND HE WILL GLADLY TELL YOU. JAMES 1:5

CREATE IN ME A PURE HEART, O GOD, AND RENEW
A STEADFAST SPIRIT WITHIN ME. PS. 51:10

IF ANYONE IS IN CHRIST, HE IS A NEW CREATION;
THE OLD HAS GONE, THE NEW HAS COME! 2 COR. 5:17

CAST YOUR CARES ON THE LORD
AND HE WILL SUSTAIN YOU. PS. 55:22

THE LORD YOUR GOD IS WITH YOU, HE IS MIGHTY TO
SAVE. HE WILL TAKE GREAT DELIGHT IN YOU, HE WILL
QUIET YOU WITH HIS LOVE. ZEPH. 3:17

THE LORD IS FAITHFUL TO ALL HIS PROMISES
AND LOVING TOWARD ALL HE HAS MADE. PS. 145:13

IN YOU, O LORD, DO I PUT MY TRUST. PS. 71:1

"BE STRONG AND COURAGEOUS. . . . THE LORD YOUR GOD WILL BE WITH YOU WHEREVER YOU GO." JOSH. 1:9

DEPEND ON THE LORD IN WHATEVER YOU DO,
AND YOUR PLANS WILL SUCCEED. PROV. 16:3

SINCE WE HAVE BEEN JUSTIFIED THROUGH FAITH,
WE HAVE PEACE WITH GOD THROUGH OUR
LORD JESUS CHRIST. ROM. 5:1

THE LORD IS MY ROCK, MY FORTRESS AND MY DELIVERER;
MY GOD IS MY ROCK, IN WHOM I TAKE REFUGE. PS. 18:2

THE WORD OF THE LORD IS RIGHT AND TRUE;
HE IS FAITHFUL IN ALL HE DOES. PS. 33:4

THE LORD IS MY STRENGTH, MY SHIELD FROM EVERY
DANGER. I TRUST IN HIM WITH ALL MY HEART. PS. 28:7

IN HIM WE HAVE REDEMPTION THROUGH HIS BLOOD,
THE FORGIVENESS OF SINS, IN ACCORDANCE WITH
THE RICHES OF GOD'S GRACE. EPH. 1:7

I TRUST IN YOUR UNFAILING LOVE. I WILL REJOICE
BECAUSE YOU HAVE RESCUED ME. PS. 13:5

LIVE A LIFE OF LOVE, JUST AS CHRIST LOVED US AND
GAVE HIMSELF UP FOR US. EPH. 5:2

"YOU WILL CALL UPON ME AND COME AND PRAY TO ME, AND
I WILL LISTEN TO YOU. YOU WILL SEEK ME AND FIND ME
WHEN YOU SEEK ME WITH ALL YOUR HEART." JER. 29:12–13

MY SOUL FINDS REST IN GOD ALONE;
MY SALVATION COMES FROM HIM. PS. 62:1

DELIGHT YOURSELF IN THE LORD, AND HE WILL
GIVE YOU THE DESIRES OF YOUR HEART. PS. 37:4

THE LORD IS MY LIGHT AND MY SALVATION—WHOM
SHALL I FEAR? THE LORD IS THE STRONGHOLD OF MY
LIFE—OF WHOM SHALL I BE AFRAID? PS. 27:1

THE LORD HIMSELF GOES BEFORE YOU AND WILL
BE WITH YOU; HE WILL NEVER LEAVE YOU NOR
FORSAKE YOU. DEUT. 31:8

GOD IS WORKING IN YOU, GIVING YOU THE DESIRE TO
OBEY HIM AND THE POWER TO DO WHAT PLEASES HIM.

PHIL. 2:13

I CAN DO EVERYTHING THROUGH CHRIST, WHO
GIVES ME STRENGTH. PHIL. 4:13

IF YOU WANT TO KNOW WHAT GOD WANTS YOU TO DO,
ASK HIM, AND HE WILL GLADLY TELL YOU. JAMES 1:5

CREATE IN ME A PURE HEART, O GOD, AND RENEW
A STEADFAST SPIRIT WITHIN ME. PS. 51:10

IF ANYONE IS IN CHRIST, HE IS A NEW CREATION;
THE OLD HAS GONE, THE NEW HAS COME! 2 COR. 5:17

CAST YOUR CARES ON THE LORD
AND HE WILL SUSTAIN YOU. PS. 55:22

THE LORD YOUR GOD IS WITH YOU, HE IS MIGHTY TO
SAVE. HE WILL TAKE GREAT DELIGHT IN YOU, HE WILL
QUIET YOU WITH HIS LOVE. ZEPH. 3:17

THE LORD IS FAITHFUL TO ALL HIS PROMISES
AND LOVING TOWARD ALL HE HAS MADE. PS. 145:13

IN YOU, O LORD, DO I PUT MY TRUST. PS. 71:1

"BE STRONG AND COURAGEOUS. . . . THE LORD YOUR GOD
WILL BE WITH YOU WHEREVER YOU GO." JOSH. 1:9

DEPEND ON THE LORD IN WHATEVER YOU DO,
AND YOUR PLANS WILL SUCCEED. PROV. 16:3

SINCE WE HAVE BEEN JUSTIFIED THROUGH FAITH,
WE HAVE PEACE WITH GOD THROUGH OUR
LORD JESUS CHRIST. ROM. 5:1

THE LORD IS MY ROCK, MY FORTRESS AND MY DELIVERER;
MY GOD IS MY ROCK, IN WHOM I TAKE REFUGE. PS. 18:2

"IF ANYONE WOULD COME AFTER ME, HE MUST DENY
HIMSELF AND TAKE UP HIS CROSS AND FOLLOW ME."

MATT. 16:24

THE WORD OF THE LORD IS RIGHT AND TRUE;
HE IS FAITHFUL IN ALL HE DOES. PS. 33:4

THE LORD IS MY STRENGTH, MY SHIELD FROM EVERY
DANGER. I TRUST IN HIM WITH ALL MY HEART. PS. 28:7

IN HIM WE HAVE REDEMPTION THROUGH HIS BLOOD,
THE FORGIVENESS OF SINS, IN ACCORDANCE WITH
THE RICHES OF GOD'S GRACE. EPH. 1:7

I TRUST IN YOUR UNFAILING LOVE. I WILL REJOICE
BECAUSE YOU HAVE RESCUED ME. PS. 13:5

LIVE A LIFE OF LOVE, JUST AS CHRIST LOVED US AND
GAVE HIMSELF UP FOR US. EPH. 5:2

"YOU WILL CALL UPON ME AND COME AND PRAY TO ME, AND
I WILL LISTEN TO YOU. YOU WILL SEEK ME AND FIND ME
WHEN YOU SEEK ME WITH ALL YOUR HEART." JER. 29:12–13

MY SOUL FINDS REST IN GOD ALONE;
MY SALVATION COMES FROM HIM. PS. 62:1

DELIGHT YOURSELF IN THE LORD, AND HE WILL
GIVE YOU THE DESIRES OF YOUR HEART. PS. 37:4

THE LORD IS MY LIGHT AND MY SALVATION—WHOM
SHALL I FEAR? THE LORD IS THE STRONGHOLD OF MY
LIFE—OF WHOM SHALL I BE AFRAID? PS. 27:1

THE LORD HIMSELF GOES BEFORE YOU AND WILL
BE WITH YOU; HE WILL NEVER LEAVE YOU NOR
FORSAKE YOU. DEUT. 31:8

GOD IS WORKING IN YOU, GIVING YOU THE DESIRE TO
OBEY HIM AND THE POWER TO DO WHAT PLEASES HIM.

PHIL. 2:13

I CAN DO EVERYTHING THROUGH CHRIST, WHO
GIVES ME STRENGTH. PHIL. 4:13

IF YOU WANT TO KNOW WHAT GOD WANTS YOU TO DO,
ASK HIM, AND HE WILL GLADLY TELL YOU. JAMES 1:5

CREATE IN ME A PURE HEART, O GOD, AND RENEW
A STEADFAST SPIRIT WITHIN ME. PS. 51:10

IF ANYONE IS IN CHRIST, HE IS A NEW CREATION;
THE OLD HAS GONE, THE NEW HAS COME! 2 COR. 5:17

CAST YOUR CARES ON THE LORD
AND HE WILL SUSTAIN YOU. PS. 55:22

THE LORD YOUR GOD IS WITH YOU, HE IS MIGHTY TO
SAVE. HE WILL TAKE GREAT DELIGHT IN YOU, HE WILL
QUIET YOU WITH HIS LOVE. ZEPH. 3:17

THE LORD IS FAITHFUL TO ALL HIS PROMISES
AND LOVING TOWARD ALL HE HAS MADE. PS. 145:13

IN YOU, O LORD, DO I PUT MY TRUST. PS. 71:1

"BE STRONG AND COURAGEOUS. . . . THE LORD YOUR GOD
WILL BE WITH YOU WHEREVER YOU GO." JOSH. 1:9

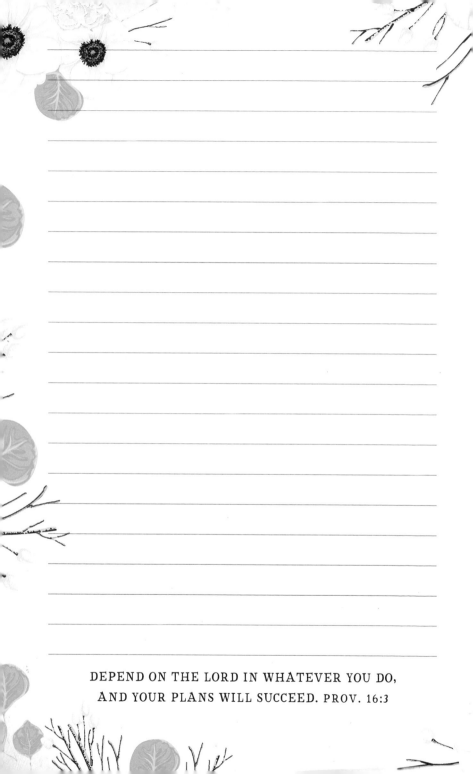

DEPEND ON THE LORD IN WHATEVER YOU DO,
AND YOUR PLANS WILL SUCCEED. PROV. 16:3

SINCE WE HAVE BEEN JUSTIFIED THROUGH FAITH,
WE HAVE PEACE WITH GOD THROUGH OUR
LORD JESUS CHRIST. ROM. 5:1

THE LORD IS MY ROCK, MY FORTRESS AND MY DELIVERER;
MY GOD IS MY ROCK, IN WHOM I TAKE REFUGE. PS. 18:2

"IF ANYONE WOULD COME AFTER ME, HE MUST DENY
HIMSELF AND TAKE UP HIS CROSS AND FOLLOW ME."

MATT. 16:24

THE WORD OF THE LORD IS RIGHT AND TRUE;
HE IS FAITHFUL IN ALL HE DOES. PS. 33:4

THE LORD IS MY STRENGTH, MY SHIELD FROM EVERY
DANGER. I TRUST IN HIM WITH ALL MY HEART. PS. 28:7

IN HIM WE HAVE REDEMPTION THROUGH HIS BLOOD,
THE FORGIVENESS OF SINS, IN ACCORDANCE WITH
THE RICHES OF GOD'S GRACE. EPH. 1:7

I TRUST IN YOUR UNFAILING LOVE. I WILL REJOICE
BECAUSE YOU HAVE RESCUED ME. PS. 13:5

LIVE A LIFE OF LOVE, JUST AS CHRIST LOVED US AND
GAVE HIMSELF UP FOR US. EPH. 5:2

_____
_____
_____
_____
_____
_____
_____
_____
_____
_____
_____
_____
_____
_____
_____
_____
_____
_____
_____
_____
_____
_____
_____
_____
_____

"YOU WILL CALL UPON ME AND COME AND PRAY TO ME, AND
I WILL LISTEN TO YOU. YOU WILL SEEK ME AND FIND ME
WHEN YOU SEEK ME WITH ALL YOUR HEART." JER. 29:12–13

MY SOUL FINDS REST IN GOD ALONE;
MY SALVATION COMES FROM HIM. PS. 62:1

DELIGHT YOURSELF IN THE LORD, AND HE WILL
GIVE YOU THE DESIRES OF YOUR HEART. PS. 37:4

THE LORD IS MY LIGHT AND MY SALVATION—WHOM
SHALL I FEAR? THE LORD IS THE STRONGHOLD OF MY
LIFE—OF WHOM SHALL I BE AFRAID? PS. 27:1

THE LORD HIMSELF GOES BEFORE YOU AND WILL
BE WITH YOU; HE WILL NEVER LEAVE YOU NOR
FORSAKE YOU. DEUT. 31:8

GOD IS WORKING IN YOU, GIVING YOU THE DESIRE TO
OBEY HIM AND THE POWER TO DO WHAT PLEASES HIM.
PHIL. 2:13

I CAN DO EVERYTHING THROUGH CHRIST, WHO
GIVES ME STRENGTH. PHIL. 4:13

IF YOU WANT TO KNOW WHAT GOD WANTS YOU TO DO,
ASK HIM, AND HE WILL GLADLY TELL YOU. JAMES 1:5

CREATE IN ME A PURE HEART, O GOD, AND RENEW
A STEADFAST SPIRIT WITHIN ME. PS. 51:10

IF ANYONE IS IN CHRIST, HE IS A NEW CREATION;
THE OLD HAS GONE, THE NEW HAS COME! 2 COR. 5:17

CAST YOUR CARES ON THE LORD
AND HE WILL SUSTAIN YOU. PS. 55:22

THE LORD YOUR GOD IS WITH YOU, HE IS MIGHTY TO
SAVE. HE WILL TAKE GREAT DELIGHT IN YOU, HE WILL
QUIET YOU WITH HIS LOVE. ZEPH. 3:17

THE LORD IS FAITHFUL TO ALL HIS PROMISES
AND LOVING TOWARD ALL HE HAS MADE. PS. 145:13

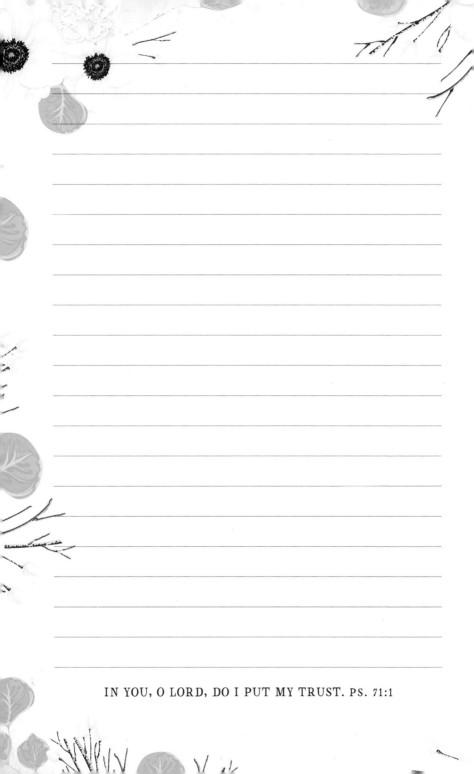

IN YOU, O LORD, DO I PUT MY TRUST. PS. 71:1

"BE STRONG AND COURAGEOUS. . . . THE LORD YOUR GOD
WILL BE WITH YOU WHEREVER YOU GO." JOSH. 1:9

DEPEND ON THE LORD IN WHATEVER YOU DO,
AND YOUR PLANS WILL SUCCEED. PROV. 16:3

SINCE WE HAVE BEEN JUSTIFIED THROUGH FAITH,
WE HAVE PEACE WITH GOD THROUGH OUR
LORD JESUS CHRIST. ROM. 5:1

THE LORD IS MY ROCK, MY FORTRESS AND MY DELIVERER;
MY GOD IS MY ROCK, IN WHOM I TAKE REFUGE. PS. 18:2

"IF ANYONE WOULD COME AFTER ME, HE MUST DENY
HIMSELF AND TAKE UP HIS CROSS AND FOLLOW ME."
MATT. 16:24

THE WORD OF THE LORD IS RIGHT AND TRUE;
HE IS FAITHFUL IN ALL HE DOES. PS. 33:4

THE LORD IS MY STRENGTH, MY SHIELD FROM EVERY
DANGER. I TRUST IN HIM WITH ALL MY HEART. PS. 28:7

IN HIM WE HAVE REDEMPTION THROUGH HIS BLOOD,
THE FORGIVENESS OF SINS, IN ACCORDANCE WITH
THE RICHES OF GOD'S GRACE. EPH. 1:7

I TRUST IN YOUR UNFAILING LOVE. I WILL REJOICE
BECAUSE YOU HAVE RESCUED ME. PS. 13:5

LIVE A LIFE OF LOVE, JUST AS CHRIST LOVED US AND
GAVE HIMSELF UP FOR US. EPH. 5:2

"YOU WILL CALL UPON ME AND COME AND PRAY TO ME, AND
I WILL LISTEN TO YOU. YOU WILL SEEK ME AND FIND ME
WHEN YOU SEEK ME WITH ALL YOUR HEART." JER. 29:12–13

MY SOUL FINDS REST IN GOD ALONE;
MY SALVATION COMES FROM HIM. PS. 62:1

DELIGHT YOURSELF IN THE LORD, AND HE WILL
GIVE YOU THE DESIRES OF YOUR HEART. PS. 37:4

THE LORD IS MY LIGHT AND MY SALVATION—WHOM
SHALL I FEAR? THE LORD IS THE STRONGHOLD OF MY
LIFE—OF WHOM SHALL I BE AFRAID? PS. 27:1

THE LORD HIMSELF GOES BEFORE YOU AND WILL
BE WITH YOU; HE WILL NEVER LEAVE YOU NOR
FORSAKE YOU. DEUT. 31:8

GOD IS WORKING IN YOU, GIVING YOU THE DESIRE TO
OBEY HIM AND THE POWER TO DO WHAT PLEASES HIM.

PHIL. 2:13

I CAN DO EVERYTHING THROUGH CHRIST, WHO
GIVES ME STRENGTH. PHIL. 4:13

IF YOU WANT TO KNOW WHAT GOD WANTS YOU TO DO,
ASK HIM, AND HE WILL GLADLY TELL YOU. JAMES 1:5

CREATE IN ME A PURE HEART, O GOD, AND RENEW
A STEADFAST SPIRIT WITHIN ME. PS. 51:10

IF ANYONE IS IN CHRIST, HE IS A NEW CREATION;
THE OLD HAS GONE, THE NEW HAS COME! 2 COR. 5:17

CAST YOUR CARES ON THE LORD
AND HE WILL SUSTAIN YOU. PS. 55:22

THE LORD YOUR GOD IS WITH YOU, HE IS MIGHTY TO
SAVE. HE WILL TAKE GREAT DELIGHT IN YOU, HE WILL
QUIET YOU WITH HIS LOVE. ZEPH. 3:17

THE LORD IS FAITHFUL TO ALL HIS PROMISES
AND LOVING TOWARD ALL HE HAS MADE. PS. 145:13

IN YOU, O LORD, DO I PUT MY TRUST. PS. 71:1

"BE STRONG AND COURAGEOUS. . . . THE LORD YOUR GOD
WILL BE WITH YOU WHEREVER YOU GO." JOSH. 1:9

DEPEND ON THE LORD IN WHATEVER YOU DO,
AND YOUR PLANS WILL SUCCEED. PROV. 16:3

SINCE WE HAVE BEEN JUSTIFIED THROUGH FAITH,
WE HAVE PEACE WITH GOD THROUGH OUR
LORD JESUS CHRIST. ROM. 5:1

THE LORD IS MY ROCK, MY FORTRESS AND MY DELIVERER;
MY GOD IS MY ROCK, IN WHOM I TAKE REFUGE. PS. 18:2

"IF ANYONE WOULD COME AFTER ME, HE MUST DENY
HIMSELF AND TAKE UP HIS CROSS AND FOLLOW ME."
MATT. 16:24

THE WORD OF THE LORD IS RIGHT AND TRUE;
HE IS FAITHFUL IN ALL HE DOES. PS. 33:4

THE LORD IS MY STRENGTH, MY SHIELD FROM EVERY
DANGER. I TRUST IN HIM WITH ALL MY HEART. PS. 28:7

IN HIM WE HAVE REDEMPTION THROUGH HIS BLOOD,
THE FORGIVENESS OF SINS, IN ACCORDANCE WITH
THE RICHES OF GOD'S GRACE. EPH. 1:7

I TRUST IN YOUR UNFAILING LOVE. I WILL REJOICE
BECAUSE YOU HAVE RESCUED ME. PS. 13:5

LIVE A LIFE OF LOVE, JUST AS CHRIST LOVED US AND
GAVE HIMSELF UP FOR US. EPH. 5:2

"YOU WILL CALL UPON ME AND COME AND PRAY TO ME, AND
I WILL LISTEN TO YOU. YOU WILL SEEK ME AND FIND ME
WHEN YOU SEEK ME WITH ALL YOUR HEART." JER. 29:12–13

MY SOUL FINDS REST IN GOD ALONE;
MY SALVATION COMES FROM HIM. PS. 62:1

DELIGHT YOURSELF IN THE LORD, AND HE WILL
GIVE YOU THE DESIRES OF YOUR HEART. PS. 37:4

THE LORD IS MY LIGHT AND MY SALVATION—WHOM
SHALL I FEAR? THE LORD IS THE STRONGHOLD OF MY
LIFE—OF WHOM SHALL I BE AFRAID? PS. 27:1

THE LORD HIMSELF GOES BEFORE YOU AND WILL
BE WITH YOU; HE WILL NEVER LEAVE YOU NOR
FORSAKE YOU. DEUT. 31:8

GOD IS WORKING IN YOU, GIVING YOU THE DESIRE TO
OBEY HIM AND THE POWER TO DO WHAT PLEASES HIM.

PHIL. 2:13

I CAN DO EVERYTHING THROUGH CHRIST, WHO
GIVES ME STRENGTH. PHIL. 4:13

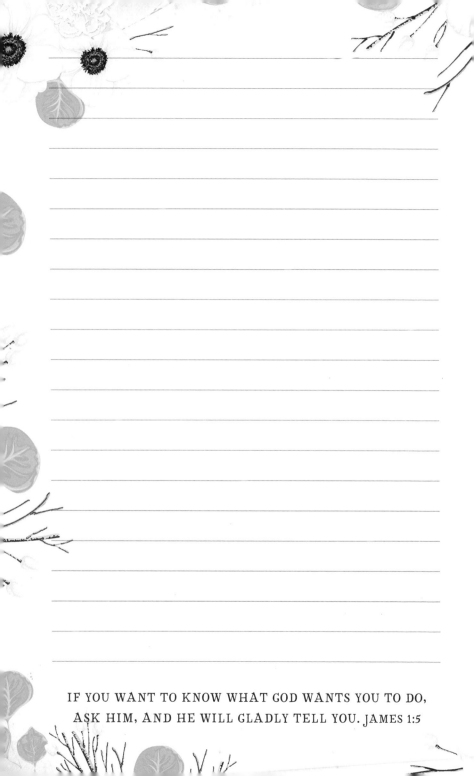

IF YOU WANT TO KNOW WHAT GOD WANTS YOU TO DO, ASK HIM, AND HE WILL GLADLY TELL YOU. JAMES 1:5

CREATE IN ME A PURE HEART, O GOD, AND RENEW
A STEADFAST SPIRIT WITHIN ME. PS. 51:10

IF ANYONE IS IN CHRIST, HE IS A NEW CREATION;
THE OLD HAS GONE, THE NEW HAS COME! 2 COR. 5:17

CAST YOUR CARES ON THE LORD
AND HE WILL SUSTAIN YOU. PS. 55:22

THE LORD YOUR GOD IS WITH YOU, HE IS MIGHTY TO
SAVE. HE WILL TAKE GREAT DELIGHT IN YOU, HE WILL
QUIET YOU WITH HIS LOVE. ZEPH. 3:17

THE LORD IS FAITHFUL TO ALL HIS PROMISES
AND LOVING TOWARD ALL HE HAS MADE. PS. 145:13

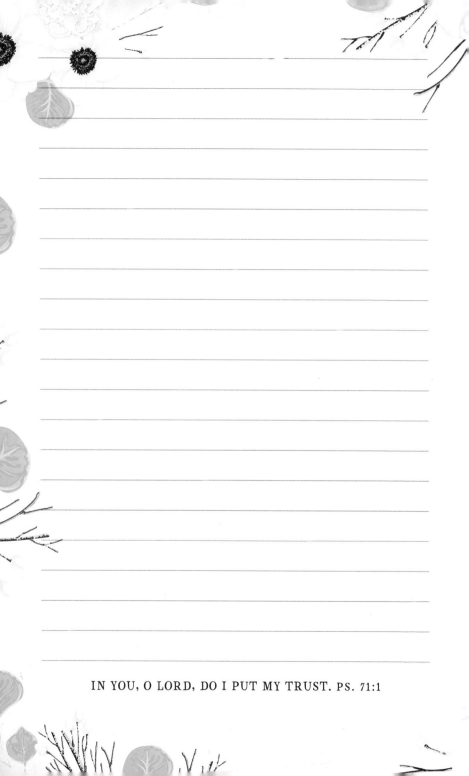

IN YOU, O LORD, DO I PUT MY TRUST. PS. 71:1

"BE STRONG AND COURAGEOUS. . . . THE LORD YOUR GOD
WILL BE WITH YOU WHEREVER YOU GO." JOSH. 1:9

DEPEND ON THE LORD IN WHATEVER YOU DO,
AND YOUR PLANS WILL SUCCEED. PROV. 16:3

SINCE WE HAVE BEEN JUSTIFIED THROUGH FAITH,
WE HAVE PEACE WITH GOD THROUGH OUR
LORD JESUS CHRIST. ROM. 5:1

THE LORD IS MY ROCK, MY FORTRESS AND MY DELIVERER;
MY GOD IS MY ROCK, IN WHOM I TAKE REFUGE. PS. 18:2

"IF ANYONE WOULD COME AFTER ME, HE MUST DENY
HIMSELF AND TAKE UP HIS CROSS AND FOLLOW ME."

MATT. 16:24

THE WORD OF THE LORD IS RIGHT AND TRUE;
HE IS FAITHFUL IN ALL HE DOES. PS. 33:4

THE LORD IS MY STRENGTH, MY SHIELD FROM EVERY
DANGER. I TRUST IN HIM WITH ALL MY HEART. PS. 28:7

IN HIM WE HAVE REDEMPTION THROUGH HIS BLOOD,
THE FORGIVENESS OF SINS, IN ACCORDANCE WITH
THE RICHES OF GOD'S GRACE. EPH. 1:7

I TRUST IN YOUR UNFAILING LOVE. I WILL REJOICE
BECAUSE YOU HAVE RESCUED ME. PS. 13:5

LIVE A LIFE OF LOVE, JUST AS CHRIST LOVED US AND
GAVE HIMSELF UP FOR US. EPH. 5:2

"YOU WILL CALL UPON ME AND COME AND PRAY TO ME, AND
I WILL LISTEN TO YOU. YOU WILL SEEK ME AND FIND ME
WHEN YOU SEEK ME WITH ALL YOUR HEART." JER. 29:12–13

MY SOUL FINDS REST IN GOD ALONE;
MY SALVATION COMES FROM HIM. PS. 62:1